Trumps Dumps: Outrageous Donald Trump Quotes that could Sway your Presidential Vote

Michael Joshua

Get a FREE copy of the eBook:

America Speaks! Real Comments Posted about Donald Trump

(www.managementtrainingonline.net/americaspeaks.html)

CONTENTS

Table of Contents

Michael Joshua

1 INTRODUCTION

There's an old saying that claims that, "Actions speak louder than words." While the gist of this statement evolves around the need for one to support his/ her words with actions, this saying can be a little misleading.

Yes, a person's actions are a major indicator of a person's state of mind, but so are the words that come out of a person's mouth. You can learn so much by things a person says alone.

The things a person says is an indication of how that person thinks. If you want to know what a person's mindset is, then all you have to do is listen to them.

Words Convey so Much

Now, a little caution must be taken. A person can say one thing and do another, yet generally speaking, you can judge a person's character by the language he/she uses, especially if taken in context.

Words have meaning, and this meaning is derived from the speaker. So, if you want to learn about a person, consider what they have said and consider them in various contexts.

Politics and Spin Doctoring

Take the political arena, for example. Listening to a political candidate's speech may give you some indication as to his/ her views on certain issues. Yet, this view is going to be limited and selective.

Most politicians are careful to only say enough to be considered as approaching the topic without having to be nailed down to a specific stance.

This spin-doctoring is why you need to consider a politician's words in various contexts. What does he/ she say when not on the grand stand? What has he/she been quoted or saying in other contexts?

These moments of insight are the moments when the candidate's real opinions show through.

The Exceptions to the Rule

Of course, while saying that most politicians guard their words, it must be admitted that there exists a rare few who speak his/her mind no matter the situation. These individuals use words on a different level than most political candidate.

While you may be thinking that speaking out in such a manner takes courage, it may just be that these individuals are speaking from a different mindset than most political candidates.

It may be that he/she feels as if he/she has nothing to lose. Or, it may be that the candidate is powerful enough in arenas outside of politics and have something else to fall back on if his/her bid for office is unsuccessful.

Finally, such unique wording may simply be the offspring of the person's personality. Whatever the reasons, this type of candidate's comments reveal how that candidate thinks, and how the candidate thinks is important.

Donald Trump

Consider Donald Trump for a moment. Here is a man that has been monumentally successful in business.

When anyone mentions Donald Trump, your average American immediately thinks billionaire (and possibly a nod toward his hair). Trump's name is synonymous with real estate. Now, he's running for president.

Why Move from Business to Politics?

What causes a man that's in private business (his net worth has been estimated until recently) to want to throw his hat in a political arena that requires him to publicly disclose his finances? This question has been on the nation's mind ever since Trump announced his candidacy.

He even addressed that very question in his announcement speech and has openly admitted that he desires to be the candidate that is set apart away from the others.

Trump doesn't think of himself as a politician. No, Trump believes in himself as a businessman. He even mentions this idea in his announcement confirming his presidential candidacy.

Words are Powerful Vehicles

That speech, along with every other comment Trump has made publicly, gives one insight into how the man thinks. His words reveal his motivation, his ideology, and his business philosophy.

As to his motivation behind his presidential bid, Trump states that it's because he's successful at business when he says,

"I don't need anybody's money. I'm using my own money. I'm not using the lobbyists. I'm not using donors. I don't care. I'm really rich...I'm not even saying that's the kind of mindset, that's the kind of thinking you need for this country. So— because we got to make the country rich. It sounds crass. Somebody said, "Oh, that's crass." It's not crass." [1]

The Source of Trump's Power

So, Trump's running because he's rich and powerful. Even more to the point, this reason is why says the things he does.

Trump has been on record making startling statements that most political candidates wouldn't ever dream of making.

He feels he can do so because he doesn't have to rely on financial backers. He can speak his mind because he's not worried about someone pulling funding.

Listen to what he has Said

With all of this being said, Trump's statements, then, give us a clearer view as to his mindset than most other candidates. He doesn't feel he needs discretion, nor does he consider discretion a positive characteristic within politicians.

So, if you really want to know Donald Trump as a political candidate, consider what he has said publicly. But, don't just consider what he's said in the political arena.

Take a look at what he's said in the business arena. You need to even examine his statements made in the realm of reality TV.

You may have read about him saying *"Sadly, she's no longer a 10"* about model Heidi Klum earlier this year, but can you guess who he is talking about in the following quotes?

"If _____ can't satisfy her husband what makes her think that she can satisfy America?"

"_____'s disgusting both inside and out. You take a look at her, she's a slob. She talks like a truck driver, she doesn't have her facts, she'll say anything that comes to her mind."

"Listen you m——f——, we're going to tax you 25 percent!"

Read on to find out who he said these to.

The Purpose of this Book

The purpose of this book is to give you some insight into Donald Trump concerning his views on business and politics. By examining statements he's been quoted as saying, you will gain an understanding of Trump's ideology.

This book is not intended to be biased in any way. Trump's statements will presented both in favor and against.

The intention of this book is to present a candid depiction of Donald Trump based upon what he has said.

2 NEGOTIATING

The most logical place to begin any discussion of what Donald Trump has said is his recorded words concerning business. Obviously, Trump has had much success in his business endeavors.

He has been revered for his negotiating skills and has been considered by many of the world's premiere negotiators (he definitely thinks of himself as such).

The Trump Persona

Even with this being said, one can't help but notice that Trump is outspoken as a businessman. In addition to being known for his strong mind for business, he is also known for his unusual public persona.

His use of this persona in speaking out on various subject matters has often placed Trump in the media spotlight. He's known for making some outrageous comments that have caused others to take notice, whether in a good way or a bad way.

No doubt about it, Trump says what Trump wants to say.

Personal Brand

Trump's ability to say what he thinks even garners him a role on The Apprentice. Sure, one can say that Trump's success made him a prime candidate as host of the reality show, but he wouldn't have been as interesting as host if hadn't been for his particular use of words.

Trump's outspoken nature is part of his personal brand, which has earned him a huge fortune. Companies pay him large sums to attach his name to their ventures. This is because the name of Donald Trump is known by millions because of his success and his ability to generate press coverage through his outlandish public comments.

Run-in with the Media

While acknowledging Trump's ability to use his public personal for his own betterment, it must be recognized that Trump's free use of his tongue has brought him under constant public scrutiny, as well.

It was his public statements regarding illegal immigrants that caused The Apprentice to sever ties with him recently. He has also been blasted in the media for many of his other controversial comments, as well.

He's been involved in a public war of words with Rosie O'Donnell since 2011, which has been rekindled since his announcement of his presidential bid. The amount of press coverage that Trump receives due to his public commentary has even increased since he's making his bid for public office.

Speaking His Mind

Whether one appreciates Trump's views or rails against them, one can't help but acknowledge that he wields powerful influence within the U.S. His power is so vast that companies pay him to use his name.

While this is being said, it must be admitted that Trump doesn't always make the best use of this power. After all, one must also recognize that Trump speaks his mind.

And, often his comments are made at the expense of others. Or, these comments are so rough in nature that others tend to rise in opposition, but no matter the response, Trump says exactly what Trump wants to say.

In so doing, Trump reveals much about his views on current issues. Anyone wanting to know the mettle of Trump the presidential candidate needs to consider his public comments and should begin with his comments on negotiating since he's been involved in that arena longer than politics.

3 NEGOTIATING IN A FAVORABLE LIGHT

If anything, Donald Trump is a man that's sure of his position in the world and aware of his capabilities. Not only is he aware of his own abilities, he lets everyone know that he's aware.

He often comments on himself publicly. His own success very well may be his favorite subject. Another area of expertise for Trump is negotiating, and he is very sure of himself in this area.

Some may even consider his pride in his own accomplishments as a close relative to arrogance. Whether you belong to this camp or not, Trump's comments provide you with a front row seat for the spectacle that is Donald Trumps' personality and character.

By reflecting upon these two favorite subjects of Trump, one a view of the kind of man Donald Trump is.

Below are only a few of Trumps more memorable statements regarding his power of negotiating.

1.   *"Love him or hate him, Trump is a man who is certain about what he wants and sets out to get it not holds barred. Women find his power almost as much of a turn-on as his money."* [2]

One can't help but see from this statement that Trump has a strong sense of self-confidence. He also believes in himself as a powerful force to be reckoned with.

He is willing to do whatever it takes to get the job done. This self-confidence is the cornerstone of his personal brand as The Donald.

While some may find this bravado abrasive, Trump has proven himself capable of backing it up. He was able to turn around a financial disaster in the 1980s to make huge gains in the late 1990s. It is this ability to achieve results that forms the basis of Trump's self-confidence.

2.   *"I've always been a fan of Steve Jobs, especially after watching Apple collapse w/out him, but the yacht he built is truly ugly."* [3]

Trump recognized that the power of one person can either bring success or failure to a venture.

Trump recognized that it was Jobs that brought success to Apple, and it was Jobs' leaving that led to Apple's financial losses. A strong leader can do much for a company or a country.

3.   *"I don't do it for the money. I've got enough, much more than I'll ever need. I do it to do it. Deals are my art form."* [4]

There's no doubt that Trump is the master of negotiating. He has the skills to negotiate tricky deals.

Such negotiations occur in the Oval Office routinely. Trump believes that these negotiating skills that have made him successful in business will make him successful in public office.

4.   *"I have made the tough decisions, always with an eye toward the bottom line. Perhaps it's time America was run like a business."* [5]

Trump is relying upon his experience as a real estate mogul as the basis of his qualifications for running for President. He believes that the government should be run like a business.

In this vein, the President should act more as a CEO than a politician.

5.   *"My Twitter has become so powerful that I can actually make my enemies tell the truth."* [6]

Trump realizes the power of social media in America's current context. Trump is very active on Twitter. He uses social media as more than a tool. He uses it as a weapon.

As soon as someone offers a negative press comment, Trump immediately comments on Twitter. He's aware of the role that public image plays in politics. He actively works to control his public image.

6.　　　*"I'm a businessman. I contribute to everybody,"* Trump said. *"When I needed Hillary, she was there. If I say 'go to my wedding,' they go to my wedding."* [7]

In this quote, Trump, during an interview, was answering a question as to why he had previously supported Hillary Clinton. Trump's reply was that his choice to support Clinton was a business decision.

He needed her status to be associated with his status. Trump recognized the need to be associated with powerful people.

7.　　　*"Hey, if you want a nice, easy, OK life, you can be in the pack ... but if you really want to do something, you do have to get out of the pack."* [8]

Trump made this statement during a promotional video for ACN, a marketing firm that he backs. He's made millions off of giving speeches for the company.

Trump has taken the position that he's different than all of the other presidential candidates in that he's not a politician. He's riding on the fact that he's an outsider within the political arena.

He has asserted in other public comments that the nation's capital needs fresh blood, and that he is the embodiment of the new perspective that our government needs.

8.　　　*"I always go into the deal anticipating the worst. If you plan for the worst — if you can live with the worst — the good will always take care of itself."* [9]

This is a quote taken from Trump's book The Art of the Deal. In this section of the book, Trump is discussing hedging your bets by only making deals that you can afford to walk away from if the situation turns negative.

Trump has acted on this principle over and over with various ventures that didn't turn out the right way, and he has been able to walk away from each one without taking a major hit.

The one exception to this being the USFL team that he purchased when the league didn't stand a chance of surviving. Trump even admits that purchase was a costly mistake.

From a leadership perspective, creating a plan of action based on worst case scenarios is intelligent. It provides a means of being prepared for any subsequent fallout. Also, it provides for any contingencies that might arise.

9.   *"Trump Tower is a building the critics were skeptical about before it was built, but which the public obviously liked. I'm not talking about the sort of person who inherited money 175 years ago and lives on 84th Street and Park Avenue. I'm talking about the wealthy Italian with the beautiful wife and the red Ferrari. Those people — the audience I was after — came to Trump Tower in droves."* [10]

Once again, this quote comes from Trump's book. The point that Trump is trying to make is that he went into Trump Tower knowing who would be interested in the building.

Trump claims that he knows his audience. He understands the individuals involved in his ventures.

10.   *"I don't hire a lot of number-crunchers, and I don't trust fancy marketing surveys. I do my own surveys and draw my own conclusions."* [11]

In the midst of discussing polls and public opinion surveys, Trump asserts that he takes his own surveys. He goes further to state that he takes a personal interest in determining public opinion in a given venture.

It is wise to take into consideration public opinion and suggestions made by others, but a wise leader also must be willing to make a firm choice and stand by that choice with conviction.

11.   *"As an entrepreneur, I choose my teachers carefully, very carefully. I am extremely cautious of the people with whom I spend my time and to whom I listen."* [12]

No successful person is successful due to his/her own efforts alone. Trump realizes this with this statement.

He also realizes that successful people are careful in selecting the people with whom they associate. Trump seeks advice from people in whom he can trust.

Having So Much to Say

As you can see, Trump has much to say on negotiating and business. He's been a leader in the field for several decades. His statements are backed by his experience.

He's made some outrageous claims, but he's also accomplished some grand feats. The quotes provided above are but a sample of the more positive comments Trump has made concerning business and negotiating.

The next chapter will look at some comments on the same topic that were made by Trump that might make a person cautious when considering Trump as a political candidate.

4 TRUMP ON NEGOTIATING: A LESS THAN FAVORABLE OPINION

Since it's been stated already that Donald Trump is known for making outlandish statements, it does no good to rehash that topic. Needless to say, Trump has made some brash statements in the past regarding business that has made him the target of many in the media.

Most often, these statements come after Trump's business activity comes into question. It might be worth examining these statements considering that Trump is balancing his candidacy on the hinge of his business success.

The following are some prime examples of Trump's statements regarding business that have come under fire in public opinion.

1.   *"I have used the laws of this country ... the [bankruptcy] chapter laws, to do a great job for my company, for myself, for my employees, for my family."* [13]

When Trump's past filings for corporate bankruptcy was questioned, he stated that he made use of the government's bankruptcy provisions as a business move. He believes that the laws were created for businesses to use them, and a business that does so is only using means that the government has provided to help them out of a poor business situation.

He doesn't feel that he was taking advantage of the situation. He claims that businesses do it all of the time. For him, using Chapter 11 is simply doing business.

2.   *"I don't like the word admire."* [14]

When asked about which business leaders did he look up to and admire, Trump stated that he doesn't admire any business leaders. Trump's ego doesn't allow him to consider other business leaders to be of the same caliber as himself.

He claims to have no business models upon which he bases his operation. In essence, his business acumen is self-invented.

3.   *"The final key to the way I promote is bravado. I play to people's fantasies. People may not always think big themselves, but they can still get very excited by those who do. That's why a little hyperbole never hurts."* [15]

Here is yet another quote from his book, The Art of the Deal. Trump is basically, within this quote, admitting to over-exaggerating publicly so as to entice the public in his favor.

Instead of letting facts speak for themselves, Trump instead puffs things up so that he can make a bigger splash. Instead of addressing reality, he plays to fantasies.

4.   *"I will be releasing the full interview with a guy named Baxter @antbaxter only to show the bias and stupidity of him and @BBCWorld. Clowns!"* [16]

Trump is notorious for using his Twitter feed for lambasting anyone who speaks out against him. In this Twitter post, Trump is giving it to a British reporter who questioned Trump's golf venture in Scotland.

He not only posts the interview, but he gives out the man's Twitter account while calling him "stupid" and referring to BBCWorld as "clowns". Trump obviously can't take criticism.

5.   *"I don't frankly have time for total political correctness. And to be honest you, this country doesn't have time either."* [17]

Trump made this statement during a Republican debate hosted by Fox News. Trump then goes on to make rude comments about China and Mexico. He even makes rude comments about the host of the debate Megyn Kelly.

Trump believes that the problems within the U.S. are too important and too serious to waste time mincing words. He believes in calling it as he sees it, no matter who it offends.

As a businessman, you think he would understand the need for discretion and how the lack of it destroys a person's public image.

6.   *"Free trade is terrible. Free trade can be wonderful if you have smart people. But we have stupid people."* [18]

Here is an example of a common tactic of Trump's. He starts by making a shocking statement. He then reverses track and amends what he says.

In this quote, he begins by saying that "free trade is terrible". He follows that up with stating that free trade could be better if the U.S. had better leaders who understand free trade because "we have stupid people".

What began as a bashing of free trade turned into a slam against incumbent politicians.

7.   *"Sorry folks, but Donald Trump is far richer and much better looking than dopey @mcuban."* [19]

Once again, Trump was taking on another business tycoon on Twitter. This time it was Mark Cuban in 2013.

Trump seems to think that business success comes down to how much money a person has and how they look. The opportunity for negotiating turned into an elementary level, social media-driven name calling session.

8. *"I promise not to talk about your massive plastic surgeries that didn't work." [20]*

It seems that the best source for Trump quips comes from Twitter. Here again is another Twitter rant. Cher is the recipient of this verbal lashing.

Cher had tweeted that she wouldn't shop at Macy's again because the chain sold the Trump clothing line. Instead of taking the high road to garner more business, Trump instead blasts Cher on Twitter.

9. *"And did you notice that baby was crying through half of the speech and I didn't get angry? Not once. Did you notice that? That baby was driving me crazy. I didn't get angry once because I didn't want to insult the parents for not taking the kid out of the room!" [21]*

A baby was crying during Trump's speech. Afterwards, he remarks on how he kept his cool and didn't get angry because the parents didn't take the baby out.

Trump obviously feels that should be commended on his restraint when he should be chastised for getting upset at a baby. Trump had made earlier comments about knowing his audience.

He obviously wasn't in touch with this one because he got upset at a baby crying during his speech.

10. *"One thing I've learned about the press is that they're always hungry for a good story, and the more sensational the better. ... The point is that if you*

are a little different, or a little outrageous, or if you do things that are bold or controversial, the press is going to write about you." [22]

While other people are trying to spin doctor public image and control what is said in the press about them, Donald Trump looks for media controversy.

More than that, he relishes in it. Trump has established his brand on sensationalism. His past performance is a good indicator of what his behavior would be like in the Oval Office.

11.   *"I know the smartest negotiators in the world. I know the good ones, I know the bad ones, I know the overrated ones. You got a lot of them that are overrated. They're not good, they think they are, they get good stories, 'cause the newspapers get buffaloed. But they're not good. But I know the best negotiators in the world. I'd put them one for each country. Believe me, folks, we'd do very well."* [23]

This statement from Trump's presidential campaign announcement seems to start off on the right foot, but then seems to go nowhere. Trump spins his wheels on the various types of negotiators that he knows.

Once he finally gets around to actually discussing negotiating, he details his plan of using a good negotiator for each country that he'd negotiate with, and that's the end of his diplomacy negotiating plan.

12.   *"You can't even use the word 'Christmas' anymore...Macy's doesn't use the word 'Christmas.'"* [24]

In a magazine article, Trump was ranting about the state of political correctness in the U.S when issued this quote. The shocking portion of this statement is the statement he makes about Macy's.

A Macy's representative denied the claim in a rebuttal. This statement is shocking because the Trump brand of clothing sells at Macy's.

It appears that Trump's opponents aren't the only target for his verbal onslaught; he rages against those with whom he has a business relationship, too.

13.   *"For the most part, you can't respect people because most people aren't worthy of respect."* [25]

This quote sums up Trump's view of other people. He doesn't even feel the majority of the country is worthy of his respect.

This is his opinion of the people that he wants to lead. This statement nullifies any other statement Trump could make about the citizens of the U.S.

Is This the Voice of America?

No one who is aware of current events can deny that Trump has his fair share of negative publicity. He's known for his outlandish statements, whether these are made in print, on television, or through social media.

He's synonymous with harsh comments. Since this is the image that Trump portrays to the world, the question remains as to whether this is the image that Trump will portray to the world if elected president.

In other words, can Trump shed his brand for the sake of the public image that the citizens of the United States expect out of their president?

Yet, considering Trump's comments regarding business is not enough to base a decision of whether or not to vote for him. He is involved in a political race, and a potential supporter must consider Trump's politics and ideology.

Unfortunately, Trump is new to politics and does not have any prior experience upon which a support can hang a decision. Instead, what Trump provides for the inquiring mind is the same type of comments that he's made as a businessman that he is now making only in regards to politics.

So, to develop a more accurate depiction of Trump's character and ethical makeup, you must consider both Trump's public comments as a businessman and as a first time politician.

5 TRUMP ON POLITICS/IDEOLOGY

Since Trump is a new player in the political game, some concern exists amongst the populous as to his position on important issues. Some are even questioning Trump's ability to speak knowledgeably on such topics because he doesn't have the political experience.

Not only do people question Trump's experience, but Trump's opponents have outright attacked his lack of political background.

While others may lament Trump's lack of political experience, Trump himself seems to revel in it. He takes pride in the fact that he isn't a politician. He believes that career politicians are weak.

Even more, he's expressed his belief that politicians are to blame for America's ills. He believes that the U.S. needs fresh blood in her leadership. He also believes that he is the fresh blood that the country needs by bringing a different mentality to Washington D.C.

Trump has stated that he will run the country like a business. Whether he actually believes that this course of action is what would be best for the country or it's simply another brag by The Donald has not been established as of yet. Either way, there's one fact that can be determined at this point.

And, the fact is this: for someone who lacks political experience, Donald Trump has been politically outspoken since he's announced his candidacy. Trump came out of the gate making comment after comment, and he hasn't stopped since that announcement. Nor, has he lost any steam.

On the contrary, the longer the campaign goes, the more Trump's list of shocking statements grows.

As with his noted comments in the world of business, any listener must wade through the verbal tidal wave to dig out precious nuggets of insight into the thought processes of Donald Trump. Yes, he has made some extremely negative comments. He's continued to verbally bash anyone who has the misfortune to oppose him.

His debate responses have been the subject of media coverage. His Twitter battles have made headlines. His interviews have spawned responses from opponents, commentators, and even from average citizens alike.

It must be stated that the response to Trump's public comments haven't been all negative, either. There is a large percentage of the population that appreciates and even applauds his audacity.

Recent polls show that Trump is still in the lead within Republican candidates. Whether it's outcry or accolade, Trump is gaining the attention he desires with his atypical, unpolitical political jockeying.

Whether you agree with his political ideology or you're repulsed by it, you have to admit that it's typical Trump, even if it's not the typical rambling expected of a political candidate.

From the very beginning of his campaign, Trump has declared that he's not like the other politicians. He's even said, "*I do love provoking people. There is truth to that. I love competition, and sometimes competition is provoking people. I don't mind provoking people. Especially when they're the right kind of people.*" [26]

That's exactly what Trump is doing: he's provoking people, whether it's provoking people to think honestly about the state of U.S. politics or provoking a negative response.

Trump is making waves in the political world simply by opening his mouth. He's even admitted to loving this sort of attention. Making such bold statements gives Trump a platform from which he further espouse his thoughts on the issues. For being an outsider to politics, Trump has much to say on political issues.

Sometimes, what he says contains nuggets of truth. Other times, his comments are nothing more than grandstanding. Either way, Trump is causing a stir within the current presidential campaign, and no one quite knows what the effects of this stir will have upon the political layout of the nation.

If you're interested in knowing where Trump the candidate stands on an issue, just consider his public comments. Trump, in typical Trump style, lays it all on the table.

Furthermore, Trump being his usual self lays out more on the table than would be considered appropriate by most standards of etiquette.

The following chapters contain both the positive and negative aspects of Trump's quoted comments regarding politics. By taking them together, you are afforded an upfront point of view into the ideology of Trump the candidate.

As with his business comments, his political comments will be considered from the favorable position first, then followed by a negative perspective.

6 POLITICS/ IDEOLOGY: SOME GEMS AMONGST THE MUCK

Even with Trump's comments being on the shocking side, there are some comments that Trump has made that make sense. These statements, while encased in typical Trump bravado, have a ring of truth to them.

Trump definitely pulls no punches when discussing the state of the union. Trump assumed this no-nonsense approach to politics from the beginning during his candidacy announcement speech and has continued on the same track throughout his campaign.

At times, you may have to dig deep to discover the point Trump's trying to make. Other times, his point is pretty obvious. No matter what, you're going to know where Donald Trump stands on an issue. The following quotes demonstrate the positive aspects of Trumps ideology.

1.   *"Negotiating from a position of strength is important. Having the will to follow through is fundamental. A Trump presidency will force the Iranians back to the bargaining table to make a much better deal."* [27]

Trump released this statement regarding Obama's nuclear deal with Iran. Trump believes that the deal with Iran will place the U.S. in a weakened state of security. He laments Obama's pursuit of the deal. He believes it's wrong to negotiate a deal that gives Iran an upper hand.

This quote is found toward the end of Trump's statement, and minus the bravado, the quote contains important information: any negotiation that is made on behalf of the United States needs to benefit the country. Trump believes that this deal doesn't do that, nor does Trump believe that the deal gives the U.S. any bargaining power.

2.   *"When did we beat Japan at anything? They send their cars over by the millions, and what do we do? When was the last time you saw a Chevrolet in Tokyo? It doesn't exist, folks. They beat us all the time."* [28]

The tilted trade agreements that America has with other countries is a documented fact. Most often, the agreements are stacked in favor of the other country and against the U.S. Trump believes that this lack of balance in trade agreements needs to be addressed if the U.S. is to compete in the global market.

He has declared that, if elected president, he would fight to make trade equitable for the U.S., which would mean more American products in foreign markets with an increase of sales that would lead to an increase in employment.

3.   *"I'm self-funding my campaign but lobbyists & special interests for Jeb & others are starting to do big ads—desperate! Don't believe them."* [29]

How political campaigns are funded is always a popular topic during campaigns. Campaigning is a big business venture for most candidates. The attention of lobbyists, political action committees, and special interest groups are diverted from political issues to garner support for candidates during campaigns.

Trump has stated from the beginning that he would not run that kind of campaign. He has bragged about being self-funded continuously through the early stages of his campaign.

It's one of his means of proving that he's different than other candidates, and that he's a successful businessman instead of being a politician.

4.   *"AMERICA will be working again. Businessmen > Politician. Private sector growth above all."* [30]

Stating that the country needs to be run like a business and lead by a businessman has been the corner stone for Trump's campaign.

On Twitter, Trump has continuously stated that, if elected president, he would work hard to increase the availability jobs within the nation. He also believes that there should be tax cuts for the middle class.

Trump has presented himself as a candidate that's concerned with the working class of America.

5.   *"As I have long stated, we are so tied in with China and Asia that their markets are now taking the U.S. market down. Get smart U.S.A."* [31]

In this tweet, Trump is speaking out against current U.S. trade practices with China. He believes that the U.S. should have a stronger stance in regards to trade with China that includes not relying so much on trade with China.

This statement comes in light of the recent financial instability in China that has had a major effect on the U.S. stock market. If elected president, Trump has vowed to tougher trade agreements with China that he believes will benefit the U.S.

6.   *"Boston incident is terrible. We need energy and passion, but we must treat each other with respect. I would never condone violence."* [32]

In this tweet, Trump is speaking out against the beating of a Mexican immigrant by two individuals who claimed that they gained inspiration for the act of violence from Trump's stance on illegal immigration.

After the incident, Trump went on record to clarify his previous negative comments regarding illegal immigrants, especially those coming from Mexico.

The tweet was Trump's attempt to reign in the effects his comments have made on the masses.

7.   *"Whether you like the decision or not, you have to go along with the Supreme Court. So that's the way it is."* [33]

In this quote, Trump was discussing the jailing of Kentucky County Clerk Kim Davis' going to jail for refusing to issue marriage licenses to same sex couples.

During this comment, Trump states that he supports religion, but he believes that refusing to issue marriage licenses to same sex couples is wrong because the Supreme Court has issued a ruling in favor of same sex marriage.

Trump states that whether you believe same sex marriage is right or wrong is irrelevant because the Supreme Court has upheld it.

8.   *"That's the thinking that our country needs. Take our jobs back from China and Japan and Mexico…"* [34]

Trump is speaking out of the practice of outsourcing jobs to foreign countries. Trump believes that outsourced jobs represent an employment opportunity that's been taken from American workers.

Trump believes that American companies should keep American jobs at home, and that this practice would benefit the economy.

9.   *"I'm owned by the people! I mean, I'm telling you, I'm no angel, but I'm gonna do right by them!"* [35]

In an interview with Rolling Stone, Trump claimed to be fighting for the American people. He states that this is why he is fighting against the outsourcing of American jobs.

He wants to act in the best interest of the country's citizens. He also claims that this fight for the common man is why he's so outspoken on the issues: he wants to be the voice for the masses.

10.   *"You have to be hit by a tractor, literally, a tractor, to use it, because the deductibles are so high, it's virtually useless. It's virtually useless. It is a disaster."* [36]

Among the many topics Trump discussed during his campaign announcement speech, Trump made sure to address Obamacare. After mentioning the proposed increases amongst the insurances available on the marketplace, Trump made this comment regarding his opinion on Obamacare.

Obviously, he considers the Affordable Healthcare Act as something that's in need of fixing. Not only does he consider the plan in need of overhaul, but he goes on to slam the marketplace website as a waste of funds.

11.   *"I watch the speeches of these people, and they say the sun will rise, the moon will set, all sorts of wonderful things will happen. And people are saying, "What's going on? I just want a job. Just get me a job. I don't need the rhetoric. I want a job."*[37]

Trump believes that politicians aren't addressing the issues. He believes that they skirt around the issues and make empty promises that they never intend to fill so that they get elected.

Trump also claims that Americans are fed up with the empty promises. His promise is that he's not going to run that kind of campaign. He claims to speak the truth on the issues.

He's going to stay true to his nature and call things as he sees them. He asserts that he will speak up for the population when no one else will.

12.   *"No more massive injections. Tiny children are not horses—one vaccine at a time, over time."* [38]

It appears that the current vaccination schedule for children has gotten under Trump's skin. He's claimed that, if elected, he would change the vaccination schedule. He would like to see vaccines for children spread out over time, instead of being lumped together.

He believes that too many vaccines at one time is dangerous to the welfare of children. He's even gone on record to support the belief that there is a direct correlation between vaccination and autism.

He's accused the researchers in opposition of this belief of having made up results. Trump began this vaccine campaign in 2007 apparently out of concern for the welfare of his son.

13.   *"The people that like me the best are the middle class and the poor people. The rich people hate me, it's true!...Because I think they are jealous, because I think they want to be famous."* [39]

Trump asserts that he's a hero to the working. He believes this is because of his desire to increase the number of jobs within the country. He has also gone on record stating that he would push for tax cuts for the middle class.

And, his tactic of appealing to the working class is working because his claims of increased jobs and economic incentives for the middle class hits close to home with a section of the population that is feeling the strains of economic hardship.

14.   *"I want to build up the military so nobody messes with us."* [40]

Trump has come out in various settings to be in favor of strengthening the military and supporting military issues. He believes that a stronger military will send a message to the world that the U.S. is a force to be reckoned with.

He also supports a change in the way that veteran's affairs are handled. He believes that veterans deserve better treatment than what they have been receiving.

Hitting the Major Issues

If you categorized Trump's statements, you would recognize a trend. Trump has spoken out publicly on all of the major current issues that exist within the current context of the U.S. And, he's done so in typical Trump style with outright, heavily opinionated, often criticized statements.

Because of the statements, Trump continues to stand strong in the early polls, and his campaign continues. Trump continues to lead GOP standings in the polls. This is due to his use of public comment.

7 SOME OF TRUMP'S MOST SHOCKING POLITICAL/IDEOLOGICAL STATEMENTS

While Trump's stance on key issues is resonating with a certain portion of the population, his statements are stirring up a hornet's nest amongst other sections of the population.

This is due to some of his more poignant comments that have triggered a large amount of media attention.

Catching Flack from his own Party

Democrats aren't the only ones questioning Trump's statements. Even members within the Republican Party have come out to express concern over Trump's position on issues.

Trump's own party is concerned that his stance on issues will weaken the overall GOP position and hinder the party's chance of putting its candidate in the presidential seat.

Why all of the Concern?

All of the concern over Trump's campaign revolves around some of the more negative comments Trump has made over the years. The concern over Trump's mouth doesn't even begin with his campaign.

He's made statements over the years that are remembered because of the acidity contained within these statements. For example, Trump's views on women, minorities, and immigrants have been noted as being highly offensive within the media.

Such comments causes one to question Trump's ability to lead such as diverse nation as the United States. Just how bad have Trump's comments been? Here are only a sample of some of Trump's more outrageous comments.

1.   *"It's certainly not groundbreaking news that the early victories by the women on 'The Apprentice' were, to a very large extent, dependent on their sex appeal."* [41]

Donald Trump's sexism has been duly noted for years. He's come out time and again with negative comments about women. This statement claiming that women winners on The Apprentice only one because of their sex appeal is only one example of Trump's negativity toward women.

In addition to this comment, Trump has also suggested that a certain woman reporter only had her job because of her looks. Trump has even commented on his daughter's looks! If he's not commenting on beautiful women, he openly calls his female opponents ugly.

He's verbally bashed Rosie O'Donnell and Megyn Kelly on social media. Women do not rank high in Trump's opinion.

2.   *"If Hillary Clinton can't satisfy her husband what makes her think that she can satisfy America?"* [42]

This comment on Twitter was later deleted, but it still remains at large thanks to those that screenshotted it to save it for posterity. This comment is another example of Trump's low opinion of women.

Trump is basically blaming former President Clinton's infidelity on Hillary Clinton. In Trump's opinion, Clinton would not have strayed if his wife would have done a better job of pleasing him.

Trump then goes on to equate a woman's leadership ability with her sexual prowess. This quote is highly inflammatory towards women, and it's no wonder why it was removed from his Twitter feed. It's also no wonder as to why people saved it.

3.   *"The concept of global warming was created by and for the Chinese in order to make U.S. manufacturing non-competitive."* [43]

Trump's disdain for the Chinese is no secret. Yet, to claim that the Chinese concocted the concept of global warming is stretching the limits of how far one can go to paint a nation in a negative light.

Trump's position on trade with China is well-known. He blames China's financial situation for the downturn in America's economy. He feels that favoring China with trade agreements is hurting the country.

As for global warming, if he's not blaming China for inventing the theory as a means to cripple the U.S., he outright denies the existence of the phenomenon.

4.   *"When Mexico sends its people, they're not sending the best. They're not sending you, they're sending people that have lots of problems and they're bringing those problems with us. They're bringing drugs. They're bringing crime. They're rapists. ... And some, I assume, are good people."* [44]

This statement has probably caused Trump the most trouble. It has caused Trump to lose supporters. It has caused Trump an endless barrage of negative responses.

It has caused companies to distance themselves from Trump: Macy's stopped carrying Trump-brand clothes, NBC and Telemundo will not be airing the Miss USA Pageant, and Trump will not be returning to The Apprentice.

Trump claims that all of these actions were instigated by himself for other reasons and are by no means a result of this outrageous statement.

Trump is definitely hard on illegal immigration, but saying that illegal immigrants from Mexico are rapists is going too far. Even Trump realizes at the end of this statement that what he said is explosive because he adds the comment that "some, I assume, are good people" as an afterthought.

5.   *"He's not a war hero. He's a war hero because he was captured. I like people that weren't captured, OK, I hate to tell you."* [45]

Trump made this statement about John McCain because Trump was apparently upset over the condition of veteran's affairs. He goes further to state that McCain is an individual who is in a position to make changes in this regard yet does nothing to help veterans.

While being outraged at the treatment of veterans within the U.S. might actually be appropriate, the manner in which Trump chose to do so is appalling. Insulting McCain set off a violent storm of negative responses, including negative responses from several veterans groups.

6.   *"Rosie O'Donnell's disgusting both inside and out. You take a look at her, she's a slob. She talks like a truck driver, she doesn't have her facts, she'll say anything that comes to her mind. Her show failed when it was a talk show, the ratings went very, very, very low and very bad, and she got essentially thrown off television. I mean she's basically a disaster."* [46]

As part of his ongoing feud with Rosie O'Donnell, Trump offered this rude comment regarding O'Donnell. He goes to great lengths to show how much he despises her.

This comment just adds more evidence against Trump in the court of public opinion concerning his thoughts on women. It also represents a strike against him as far as retaliation is concerned. It seems that Trump likes to throw insults at others, but can't take them when they are hurled his way.

7.   *"It's like in golf. A lot of people — I don't want this to sound trivial — but a lot of people are switching to these really long putters, very unattractive. It's weird. You see these great players with these really long putters, because they can't sink three-footers anymore. And, I hate it. I am a traditionalist. I have so many fabulous friends who happen to be gay, but I am a traditionalist."* [47]

Okay, to begin with… that's a strange analogy. Comparing homosexuality to choosing a different golf club because the golfer can't sink a short put? So, is Trump assuming that men become homosexuals due to lack of successful relationships with women?

Whatever the meaning of the analogy, Trump is basically stating that he's a traditionalist, and that he views heterosexuality as traditional. Thus, homosexuality is untraditional.

Incidentally, did Trump intentionally mean to use the word "fabulous" to describe his gay friends? Or, was he just not thinking before speaking again?

8.   *"I don't think Ivanka would do that [pose for Playboy], although she does have a very nice figure. I've said if Ivanka weren't my daughter, perhaps I'd be dating her."* [48]

It's refreshing to know that Trump won't cross the incest line. Yet, he's stopped long enough to consider whether or not he'd date Ivanka if she wasn't his daughter.

Comments like these makes a person question Trump's train of thought. There's no need for further explanation; the comment is weird enough on its own. Once again, this goes to show what he thinks about women, including his own daughter.

9.   *"The line of 'Make America great again,' the phrase, that was mine, I came up with it about a year ago, and I kept using it, and everybody's using it, they are all loving it. I don't know I guess I should copyright it, maybe I have copyrighted it."* [49]

While this is a great line, and Trump has used it, he's not the originator of it. Trump is only taking credit for coming up with it. In fact, Ronald Reagan said it before.

Just as Trump takes credit for being a self-made man when actually started off by inheriting from his father, Trump takes credit for somebody else's words.

10.   *"Listen you m——f——, we're going to tax you 25 percent!"* [50]

This comment was what Trump would say to China if he were president. While Trump may be correct in stating that the U.S. trade policy is unbalanced in favor of China, such a statement as the quote above doesn't represent great negotiating skills.

Is this a hint of the type of diplomacy that Trump would use if he won the election?

11. *"You look at Baltimore, you look at Cleveland. You look at all of those places, just exploding. We have an African-American president [and] we've never had it so bad."* [51]

Trump made this statement on Good Morning America. He was speaking about the various incidents involving police brutality against African-Americans.

Whether or not Trump meant for the comment to come off as it did, the comment seems to be stating that the problems in America are a result of having an African-American president.

12. *"I think the big problem this country has is being politically correct."* [52]

This comment was in response to Megyn Kelly's comment during a debate that Trump's Twitter feed contains numerous negative comments about certain women's appearances. This quote was Trump's reply. Despite all of the other major issues that are currently engulfing our country, Trump suggests that our country suffers from being politically correct.

Trump considers being nice and not blasting a woman's appearance on social media as being politically correct.

13. *"I'm talking about a lot of leverage. I want to win and we will win,"* [53]

During the GOP debate, the candidates were asked to raise their hands if they would not sign a pledge to support the GOP candidate if they weren't chosen to represent their party?

Trump raised both his hands and issued this statement. He then went on to say that not only would he not support the candidate, but that he would also not respect the candidate.

For Trump, it's about the competition and not about the good of the party. Of course, he eventually recanted and signed the pledge, but this was only after he received criticism for his comments.

14.   *"Islamic terrorism is eating large portions of the Mideast. They've become rich. I'm in competition with them."* [54]

Trump admits that terrorism is running amuck. Yet, he seems only to be bothered by it because the terrorists are making money.

They are competing with him financially, and this has offended him. Trump doesn't mention the horrors that are committed by terrorists. He doesn't mention the effects on the inhabitants that are under the influence of the terrorists. He's simply worried about his profit margin.

Is This a Hint of More To Come?

These statements by Donald Trump are shocking, to say the least. If one gauges Trump's politics and ideology by these statements, one can assume several things about Trump.

First of all, he has a low view of women. Secondly, he harbors some racist tendencies. Thirdly, Trump is only concerned with winning and not about the welfare of the country. The question remains as to whether these statements represent the bulk of Trump's ideology or are they isolated incidents.

Even more, one wonders whether or not Trump will make more of such comments in the future. If he is elected president, will he be constantly in the news for comments that he's made.

Such comments makes one question whether Trump will be able to respond appropriately in the face of crisis. The country looks to the president for solace, direction, and hope. If Trump is president, will the nation receive a biting remark, instead?

8 CONCLUSION

There many questions that surround the presidential candidacy of Donald Trump. Sure, he's a known figure in the world of business. Yet, leading the country is not business.

Being president is politics, and Trump is a newcomer to the political scene. Everyone's eyes are on Donald Trump as he makes his bid for the presidency. He's currently being weighed and measured to determine his mettle.

Is He Good Enough?

While there is a growing number of citizens who are turning out in favor of Trump, political analysts and politicians alike are wondering if Trump has what it takes to lead a nation.

In addition, they are wondering if he can reign in his tongue. Yes, he has made some good points. Yes, he knows what he's talking about when it comes to finances.

Yet, the old saying says that "The medium is the message." Trump needs to consider that how something is said is just as important as what is being said.

He may feel that certain comments need to be made, but he must make them at the right time and in the right attitude.

Serious Problems Need Serious Attention

Mr. Trump may be right. The U.S. does have serious problems: threats of terrorism, healthcare, Social Security, and the state of the economy are but few of the issues that are plaguing the nation.

The U.S. needs strong leadership that can guide her through these troubled waters. That leader will have to take a firm stand to address some of these issues, and that stand may not be popular.

The next president will need courage to face America's troubles head on. He/she will also have to be able to unite a country that is currently splintering. These issues can't be joked away.

To accomplish all that needs to take place to head the nation back in a positive course, the next president will have to rely upon diplomacy.

Trump's Challenge

Donald Trump's challenge is to meet these demands while staying true to his persona. If he can convince voters that he can do this, then he might have a chance of winning the election.

If he can't pull off instilling confidence in the midst of his incessant verbal hammering, then the nation might witness one of the most interesting losing campaigns in history. The outcome depends upon Trump's willingness to walk the balance between saying what needs to be said and saying something just to be heard. No one knows how this election will turn out.

No one really knows the extent to which Trump's campaign will affect the outcome in 2016. It's this uncertainty with Trump that has set some on edge. At the same time, it's his unique approach that others find refreshing. Ultimately, he has to encourage more of the latter and less of the former.

The Weight of Your Conscience

That's the dilemma that Trump faces. Your dilemma, as a voter is to determine which candidate is the right choice for you based upon your own beliefs and values.

Sure, it helps to listen to the political analysts, but in the end, they're not going to be with you in the voting booth. You're the one who decides your vote. You have to consider deeply your choice. This means that you have to be well informed regarding the candidates.

Evaluating the Given Facts

With Donald Trump, this task is not made easier. He has no political track record on which to base your decision. Instead, you must consider his performance outside of politics and his actions during the campaign.

One way in which you can evaluate Mr. Trump is by his public comments. By considering all that he has said, both in the political arena and out of the political arena, you can gain some sort of sense of his political leanings.

Then, you can compare his ideology to your belief system and determine whether or not they match. If they do, then you could vote for him in good conscience.

If Trump's ideology clashes with yours, then you might not want to vote for him so as to avoid any ethical dilemma on your part.

To Vote is to Choose

In the end, your vote symbolizes your choice. By voting for Trump you declare that you support his actions, his values, and his statements. Before casting the ballot, you need to decide whether or not you do support Trump in such a manner.

Evaluating Trump's recorded comments gives you an opportunity to do that.

This book was written to provide you with examples of the kinds of comments that Trump is notorious for. It was presented in a way that provided information without trying to lead you one way or another as far as Trump is concerned as a presidential candidate.

It would be so much easier if someone could show us the way in which we should vote. But, then again, that's not how democracy works. As a registered voter, you have an obligation to make your vote count and to ensure that your vote is an educated vote.

You can't take a vote back once you've cast it. If you realize that you've voted in error, the only thing to do is to live with the results of that election for the length of time that the person elected is in office.

Therefore, you owe it yourself to consider Trump's comments before making a decision. More than that, as part of the democratic process, you owe it to the nation to make an informed decision.

After all, the fate of the nation rests in the hands of the next president. So, consider Trump's use of the English language and make an informed decision.

9 FOOTNOTES

1. June 16, 2015 http://time.com/3923128/donald-trump-announcement-speech/

2. August 19, 2015 http://www.huffingtonpost.com/entry/18-real-things-donald-trump-has-said-about-women_55d356a8e4b07addcb442023

3. July 11, 2015 http://thoughtcatalog.com/lorenzo-jensen-iii/2015/07/50-donald-trump-quotes-that-are-so-dumb-theyll-make-your-brain-hurt/

4. July 28, 2015 http://www.inc.com/john-brandon/20-outrageous-donald-trump-quotes-on-business.html

5. July 28, 2015 http://www.inc.com/john-brandon/20-outrageous-donald-trump-quotes-on-business.html

6. http://www.refinery29.com/2015/08/91867/donald-trump-offensive-quotes#slide-12

7. July 17, 2015 http://time.com/3962799/donald-trump-hillary-clinton/

8. September 7, 2015 http://www.bloomberg.com/politics/graphics/2015-how-trump-invented-trump/

9. June 16, 2015 http://www.businessinsider.com/donald-trump-business-philosophy-from-the-art-of-the-deal-2015-6

10. June 16, 2015 http://www.businessinsider.com/donald-trump-business-philosophy-from-the-art-of-the-deal-2015-6

11. August 26, 2015 http://www.myfoxal.com/story/29887573/karles-korner-donald-trump-football-coach-he-sure-talks-like-one

12. August 24, 2015 http://www.inc.com/larry-kim/21-brilliant-quotes-from-the-donald-trump.html

13. August 31, 2015 http://money.cnn.com/2015/08/31/news/companies/donald-trump-bankruptcy/

14. September 3, 2015 http://www.bloomberg.com/politics/graphics/2015-how-trump-invented-trump/

15. August 5, 2015 http://www.ibtimes.com/pulse/donald-trump-quotes-50-best-sayings-republican-presidential-candidate-2040644

16. June 16, 2015 http://www.bustle.com/articles/90679-the-16-worst-donald-trump-quotes-are-all-the-evidence-you-need-that-hell-never-and

17. August 6, 2015 http://mashable.com/2015/08/06/donald-trump-gop-debate-quotes/

18. July 11, 2015 http://thoughtcatalog.com/lorenzo-jensen-iii/2015/07/50-donald-trump-quotes-that-are-so-dumb-theyll-make-your-brain-hurt/

19. March 13, 2013 http://www.hollywoodreporter.com/gallery/donald-trump-his-20-best-432843/5-vs-mark-cuban

20. April 4, 2013 http://www.hollywoodreporter.com/gallery/donald-trump-his-20-best-432843/8-vs-cher

21. June 16, 2015 http://wonkette.com/588547/here-are-12-of-the-stupidest-things-ever-to-come-out-of-donald-trumps-mouth-hole

22. August 14, 2015 http://www.politico.com/magazine/story/2015/08/the-absolute-trumpest-121328

23. June 16, 2015 http://www.politico.com/story/2015/06/donald-trump-2016-announcement-10-best-lines-119066

24. September 8, 2015 http://www.nydailynews.com/news/politics/trump-u-s-race-relations-bad-article-1.2351264

25. September 8, 2015 http://www.nytimes.com/2015/09/09/us/politics/donald-trump-likens-his-schooling-to-military-service-in-book.html?_r=0

26. January 6, 2015 http://www.biography.com/news/donald-trump-quotes-facts

27. September 8, 2015 http://www.usatoday.com/story/opinion/2015/09/08/donald-trump-amateur-hour-iran-nuclear-deal-column/71884090/

28. June 6, 2015 http://time.com/3923128/donald-trump-announcement-speech/

29. https://twitter.com/realDonaldTrump

30. https://twitter.com/realDonaldTrump

31. https://twitter.com/realDonaldTrump

32. https://twitter.com/realDonaldTrump

33. September 10, 2015 http://www.politico.com/story/2015/09/donald-trump-syrian-refugees-213430

34. September 9, 2015 http://www.rollingstone.com/politics/news/trump-seriously-20150909?page=3

35. September 9, 2015 http://www.usmagazine.com/celebrity-news/news/donald-trump-explains-why-voters-like-him-im-owned-by-the-people-201599

36. June 16, 2015 http://time.com/3923128/donald-trump-announcement-speech/

37. June 16, 2015 http://time.com/3923128/donald-trump-announcement-speech/

38. June 4, 2015 http://mic.com/articles/121765/10-quotes-that-show-donald-trump-will-be-the-greatest-american-president

39. June 4, 2015 http://mic.com/articles/121765/10-quotes-that-show-donald-trump-will-be-the-greatest-american-president

40. August 3, 2015 http://www.nydailynews.com/news/politics/trump-1st-order-business-prez-building-military-article-1.2312826

41. August 19, 2015 http://www.huffingtonpost.com/entry/18-real-things-donald-trump-has-said-about-women_55d356a8e4b07addcb442023

42. August 24, 2015 http://www.huffingtonpost.com/entry/18-real-things-donald-trump-has-said-about-women_55d356a8e4b07addcb442023

43. July 23, 2015 http://presidential-candidates.insidegov.com/stories/5187/23-ridiculously-offensive-donald-trump-quotes#2

44. July 23, 2015 http://presidential-candidates.insidegov.com/stories/5187/23-ridiculously-offensive-donald-trump-quotes#2

45. August 16, 2015 http://www.eonline.com/news/678223/donald-trump-s-most-absurd-sounding-comments-so-far-about-people-policy-and-a-certain-presidency

46. August 6, 2015 http://www.usmagazine.com/celebrity-news/news/donald-trumps-craziest-quotes-the-2016-presidential-hopeful-speaks-201568

47. August 6, 2015 http://www.usmagazine.com/celebrity-news/news/donald-trumps-craziest-quotes-the-2016-presidential-hopeful-speaks-201568

48. July 1, 2015 http://www.bustle.com/articles/94152-10-donald-trump-quotes-about-women-that-help-explain-why-nbc-gave-him-the-boot

49. August 6, 2015 http://www.usmagazine.com/celebrity-news/news/donald-trumps-craziest-quotes-the-2016-presidential-hopeful-speaks-201568

50. August 24, 2015 http://www.business2community.com/government-politics/23-ridiculously-offensive-donald-trump-quotes-01284968

51. September 10, 2015 http://www.wmur.com/politics/donald-trumps-most-provoking-quotes/34313688

52. August 7, 2015 http://www.theguardian.com/us-news/2015/aug/07/donald-trump-in-the-gop-debate-his-best-lines-and-the-most-cringeworthy

53. August 7, 2015 http://www.theguardian.com/us-news/2015/aug/07/donald-trump-in-the-gop-debate-his-best-lines-and-the-most-cringeworthy

54. June 16, 2015 http://www.politico.com/story/2015/06/donald-trump-2016-announcement-10-best-lines-119066

ABOUT THE AUTHOR

Michael Joshua got his undergraduate degree in Finance and works full time at a large bank as a Financial Analyst. He has great knowledge in Business & Money, along with politics and technology. This is his first published book as an author.

Goodreads:

https://www.goodreads.com/user/show/46377085-michael-joshua

www.ingramcontent.com/pod-product-compliance
Lightning Source LLC
Chambersburg PA
CBHW070940180526
45168CB00003B/1122